A special thank-you for

Kristi

You are special to me.
Thank you for your thoughtfulness.

With gratitude,

Joy

Date
_1/29/05_

the
thank
you
s e r i e s™

*O*ur purpose at Howard Publishing is to:
- *Increase faith* in the hearts of growing Christians
- *Inspire holiness* in the lives of believers
- *Instill hope* in the hearts of struggling people everywhere

Because He's coming again!

Thank You for Your Thoughtfulness © 2003 by Howard Publishing Company
All rights reserved. Printed in the United States of America

Published by Howard Publishing Co., Inc.
3117 North 7th Street, West Monroe, Louisiana 71291-2227

03 04 05 06 07 08 09 10 11 12   10 9 8 7 6 5 4 3 2

Stories by Debbie Webb
Edited by Between the Lines
Interior design by LinDee Loveland and Stephanie Denney

ISBN: 1-58229-277-9

thank you

for your
thoughtfulness

a collection of poems,
prayers, stories, quotes, and
scriptures to say thank you

HOWARD
PUBLISHING CO.

thank you for your thoughtfulness

thank you for your thoughtfulness

thank you for your thoughtfulness

thank you for your thoughtfulness

thank you fo

thank you for your thoughtful

thank you for your thoughtfulness

thank you

Your thoughtful

ways have

inspired me to

strive to be like

you—to pass on

the blessings of

thoughtfulness.

thank
you

for your
thoughtfulness

Dear _____,

   We live in a world where people have little time for acts of kindness. Most of us feel overextended, stressed, and pushed to the limit as we hurry to meet deadlines and keep up with demanding schedules. It seems our lifestyles have crowded out our availability to recognize and respond to the needs of others.

   And then there's you. It's reassuring to know that there are still people in this world who will do thoughtful things for others—things that could be overlooked easily but that make a difference in others' lives.

   You have made that kind of difference in my life, and I hope to pay tribute to your kindness with the words of this little book. Thank you for your thoughtfulness—for the generous expression of your gracious heart.

                                With deep gratitude,

Ruth
1:8

CEV

YOU HAVE ALWAYS BEEN KIND TO ME. I PRAY THAT THE LORD WILL BE JUST AS KIND TO YOU.

Nobility

True worth is in being, not seeming,
In doing, each day that goes by,
Some little good—not in dreaming
Of great things to do by and by.
For whatever men say in their blindness,
And spite of the fancies of youth,
There's nothing so kingly as kindness,
And nothing so royal as truth.

—Alice Cary

The Appointment

 *I can't believe this storm,* Madison thought as she gazed pensively out the glass door of the department store. Her umbrella was under the front passenger's seat of her car, but little good it would do her now— she was parked at least a hundred yards away. *I'll just stand here and wait until the torrent dies down, then I'll make a mad dash for that awning over there,* she thought, planning her strategy for the driest possible departure.

Normally, Madison wouldn't have cared so much about getting wet, but she had an interview this afternoon at an ad agency, and she knew her appearance mattered a great deal— possibly more than it had ever mattered in her life. Madison was a marketing major with a flair for personal presentation, and she wanted that hallmark to make a strong, positive first impression.

Madison had shopped for two hours last week, carefully selecting just the right accessories to add a touch of class to her softly polished style. She had chosen a silk scarf for her neck—tied with expert, artistic precision—and a pair of twisted hoop earrings that hung in perfect proportion to her hair length. Her ivory, raw silk suit fit her lithe frame like a glove, with an exaggerated slit up the side.

Madison really needed this job. Since graduating two months ago, her experience in a retail sales position had convinced her that she wanted to capitalize on her educational investment as quickly as possible. Madison's career aspirations and careful planning would take her on a fast track to impressive earnings if she could just break into the market. Right now, after working hard for paltry pay, landing a position and making money—lots of it—were all Madison cared about.

Fifteen minutes passed, and Madison started to feel a little anxious. She had left her job at the mall in plenty of time, pending no delays. But now, with a quarter of an hour lost, she felt the pressure of needing to head for her interview.

The Appointment

"Looks pretty soggy out there, huh?" a soft voice spoke from behind her. Madison turned to see a young woman standing with twin baby girls. She had a rented stroller, the industrial sort that carries two children and lots of shopping bags. One of the children was sleeping in the stroller; the other fidgeted restlessly in her arms.

"Are you parked out there, too?" Madison queried.

"No, my mom was supposed to pick us up nearly two hours ago, and I don't know what to think. I hope she's OK."

"I have a cell phone; would you like to call her?" Madison offered. She prided herself on her gracious gesture to foot the bill for this stranger to call her mom.

"I've tried numerous times at the pay phone," the young woman responded. "No answer. She doesn't have a cell phone. Thanks, though, that's very kind of you."

Madison took stock of the young woman trying to console the fretful baby. She seemed too young to be the mother of the twins, but her easy, loving manner with them and the way the baby responded indicated she was.

Looks like a bargain-rack outfit, Madison surmised as she evaluated the woman's clothing and shoes. *And her hair defi-*

nitely lacks a professional stylist's signature. No wedding ring. We're sure from different walks of life.

"Where do you live?" Madison ventured.

"About twelve miles south," said the young woman, "toward the city."

"I'd call a cab, if I were you, and explain to my mom later," Madison said matter-of-factly.

The young woman nodded and averted her eyes. "That's probably a good idea."

A pang of sadness stung Madison's heart as it dawned on her that this young woman couldn't afford a cab. She was stranded and helpless.

The sleeping infant suddenly awoke and started to cry, and her already restless twin joined in to create a cacophony of ear-splitting screams. The young mother's worried demeanor turned into a controlled panic as she tried unsuccessfully to quiet the babies.

She spoke apologetically over the noise: "I'm out of formula, and they're really getting hungry. I'm so sorry, I'll just go to another exit."

Madison saw a tear of frustration and fear spill onto the

The Appointment

young mother's cheek, but the woman quickly wiped it away, trying to keep her composure.

"Look," Madison started, "I'm headed your direction. Why don't I just take you home?"

What am I thinking! Madison's sense of reason shouted back at her. *I'll be late for the interview!* But the offer was spoken, and Madison knew in her heart that it was the right thing to do. Maybe the people at the agency would applaud her effort. Then again, maybe not.

"I couldn't take advantage of you like that," the young woman answered reluctantly. "You're obviously dressed for some important occasion. I'll just wait a little longer."

"Then what?" Madison countered. "Look, I have a sister with a baby, and if she were stranded, I hope someone would help her. Come on! It's high time I got out of here anyway."

Madison lifted the baby from the stroller into her silk-suited arms. The women each grabbed one of the shopping bags and headed out into the downpour. Walking as fast as she could in heels, Madison hovered over the baby to keep her dry, sacrificing any chance at keeping her hair in presentable condition.

As she ducked into the driver's seat, the baby accidentally

yanked her left earring out of her ear, sending it rolling down the drainage grate nearby. *Unbelievable!* Madison thought. *Oh well, it's just an earring,* she reminded herself. *A sixty-dollar earring, but still just an earring.*

Madison said nothing, hoping the young mother hadn't seen it. But the young woman dug through her purse, pulled out five or six one-dollar bills, and offered them to Madison. "I'm so sorry," she said.

"It was an old pair," Madison fibbed, refusing the money.

The babies were wailing louder now that they were wet and hungry. The two women tried to calm them, but to no avail. Finally, the young mother said, "Let me get Sarah situated on this side, then you can hand Hannah to me in the other arm."

At that moment, Hannah belched loudly and deposited a yellow curdle of stale formula onto Madison's ivory silk suit. The young mother gasped in horror, grabbed a burping cloth, and tried to wipe up the mess, but she only succeeded in smearing it deeper into the fabric.

Madison sat stunned for a moment at what surely would be the death of her chance at getting this job. "Don't worry," she finally said, "the dry cleaner will get it out."

The Appointment

"I'll pay for it," the young woman promised. "I'm so sorry." The barrage of discouraging events was finally more than she could bear, and she dissolved into tears.

It was in that instant that Madison's heart took over. "Listen," she said compassionately, "this is just a piece of clothing. I don't know what has happened to your mother, but I do know that you need to get home. And I believe my real mission today is to get you there. Whatever else I need to do is of little significance when compared with you and your precious little girls."

A feeling of warmth overtook Madison, and she smiled radiantly at the woman in the passenger seat. "By the way, my name is Madison. I know Sarah and Hannah. What's your name?"

"Michelle," came the soft-spoken answer. "Michelle Parker."

Madison and Michelle talked as they traveled, getting to know each other as much as possible over the next twelve miles. It was the most meaningful trip Madison could remember in a long time.

Madison helped Michelle and the twins to the door of their modest home. Then she heartily embraced all three of them.

"You take care," she said to Michelle, who now had tears of gratefulness in her eyes. "I'm so glad our paths crossed today. You've blessed my life more than you realize."

Madison stops by Michelle's house regularly on the way home from her new job at the ad agency for a cup of tea and some sweet baby kisses. She never regrets the impulse of thoughtfulness that overtook her that rainy day. Those unfortunate circumstances led to a lifelong friendship and an invaluable blessing—knowing that the seeds of thoughtfulness sown in mercy returned a harvest of abundant love.

The Appointment

thank you for your thoughtfulness

thank you for your thoughtfulness

thank you for

thank you for your thoughtfulness

thank you for your thoughtfulness

thank you for your thoughtfulnes

thank you for your thoughtfulness

thank
you

Your thoughtfulness

has touched my

heart, refreshed

my soul, and

changed my life

and the way

I hope to live it.

a blessing
for you

$\mathcal{M}$ay your generosity be felt

$\mathcal{I}$n every heart you find,

$\mathcal{A}$nd make its way back to you

$\mathcal{I}$n thoughtfulness, in kind.

for your
thoughtfulness

$\mathscr{M}$ay the compassion you've given

$\mathscr{B}$e shared in such a way,

$\mathscr{T}$hat hearts who have received

$\mathscr{R}$eflect your love each passing day.

Success in life has nothing to do with what you gain in life or accomplish for yourself. It's what you do for others.

DANNY THOMAS

thank you for your thoughtfulness

thank you for your thoughtfulness

thank you for your thoughtfulness

thank you for your thoughtfulness

thank you fo

thank you for your thoughtful

thank you for your thoughtfulness

thank
you

Like a rainbow

after a spring rain,

your thoughtfulness

has made my life

beautiful.

Little Things

Little drops of water,
Little grains of sand,
Make the mighty ocean
And the pleasant land.

Little deeds of kindness,
Little words of love,
Make our earth an Eden,
Like the heaven above.

—Julia A. Fletcher Carney

Proverbs
31:26

NKJV

SHE OPENS
HER MOUTH
WITH WISDOM,
AND ON
HER TONGUE
IS THE LAW
OF KINDNESS.

In the Company of Friends

Cheryl's cat, Moses, had been her faithful friend for thirteen years. The day he died she'd have cried a river, except for Mrs. Chandler's interruption.

Moses was an extraordinary cat. He was a Maine coon with a long, lush coat of gray and white fur, smartly accented with a dignified mane. His exaggerated, expressive eyebrows were tufted like Einstein's, and his impressive bush of a tail looked like a raccoon's. Moses was beautiful, extravagant, perhaps even a little overstated. And he was the size of a small cocker spaniel.

In fact, Moses was more like a dog than a cat. When Cheryl came home from school or work, he would run to meet her at the door, sitting on his hindquarters and raising his front paws to signal that he wanted to be picked up and hugged. He loved

In the

to ride in Cheryl's arms, looking over her shoulder like a baby, with one paw wrapped affectionately around her neck and the other resting on her shoulder, face pressed against her cheek.

Moses was a high-school graduation gift from Cheryl's parents—and not altogether a welcomed one. Cheryl wasn't sure she wanted the burden of caring for a pet. But she had since come to appreciate her parents' foresight into her need for companionship once she left home.

Throughout Cheryl's college career, she and Moses lived in a tiny apartment over a garage. The homeowner, Mrs. Chandler, had been reluctant to allow the large, furry cat to move in. But she granted a probationary period and ended up falling head over heels in love with Moses and his owner.

When Mrs. Chandler visited, typically once a week, Moses seemed to sense that it was his chance to win over his critic. He turned all his feline charm toward the elderly woman. First he stalked her, flirtatiously eyeing her as he walked across the back of the couch. Next, he'd walk close by, wrapping his soft tail around her legs and letting it stroke her ankles. Then he'd look up, innocent and irresistible. Finally, he'd pounce onto her lap and rub his head affectionately against her chin. Soon he'd be

Company of Friends

curled snugly on her lap, purring like a tractor. Moses and Mrs. Chandler were tight.

Eight years had passed between Cheryl and Moses in the tiny apartment. Cheryl experienced the exuberance of first love and the anguish of a broken heart, while Moses gave consistent affection and comfort. Cheryl experienced the stress of her first real job and the exhilaration of success; Moses held steady through each peak and valley.

For eight years Mrs. Chandler petted Moses on her front porch when he stopped by on his early morning stroll and again in the evening. And life passed by routinely for Cheryl, Moses, and Mrs. Chandler.

That is, until the day Moses developed a cough. Cheryl called on Mrs. Chandler, inquiring whether she had ever heard a cat cough. She could tell by her silence that Mrs. Chandler was concerned. She said, "Honey, let me take a look at him. I haven't seen the old coot in a couple of days; I need to come pat him on the head anyway."

Moses greeted Mrs. Chandler, however, not with his usual finesse. He completely bypassed the formalities and went straight for her lap. She noticed that his eyes lacked their usual luster, and he graced her lap for a full hour before she got up to leave.

Moses was diagnosed with feline leukemia. With tears streaming down her face, Cheryl told Mrs. Chandler of his condition. He would likely live only a couple more weeks. Mrs. Chandler wrapped her thin, wrinkled arm around her young friend's shoulders and tried to comfort her. "Honey, Moses has had the happiest life any cat could imagine looking after you. Don't let him know that you're sad or he'll think he's falling down on the job. Let him believe nothing's changed, and enjoy the time you have together. You can cry when he's not around to see it." Mrs. Chandler picked up Moses and held him for a long time. Purring softly, he did his best to show affection for his old friend.

Mrs. Chandler offered to care for Moses during the day while Cheryl was at work. The faithful feline spent his last days curled for hours on end on the kind woman's lap. His evenings were spent with his devoted friend Cheryl, who set aside her tears to enjoy their last happy moments together. On Sunday, while stretched out across Cheryl's bed like a prince on his couch, Moses died quietly and with dignity. Cheryl was with him, just as she always had been.

Company of Friends

An hour after Moses died, Cheryl's doorbell rang. With eyes swollen from crying, Cheryl opened the door to find the old woman holding a tiny, squirming ball of feline fur! "You won't believe what showed up on my doorstep..." Mrs. Chandler explained. "You're the only one I can think of who will take him in. By the way," she continued, "I named him Joshua. As for Moses, let's give him a proper burial."

That afternoon, the two women worked side by side in the backyard, digging a grave. They lowered the object of their shared grief, wrapped in a soft blanket, into the grave and filled in the dirt. Silently and lovingly, they tucked a bouquet of wildflowers into the moist sod. Then, arm in arm, the two women returned to the house to answer the tender mewing of a fresh life.

There wasn't much time for crying in the days that followed— Cheryl was busy tending to tiny Joshua. Without her realizing it, he filled her days and occupied her heart where Moses had left off.

Two years later, as Cheryl stood at a graveside service for Mrs. Chandler, she pondered the unique and precious friendship they had discovered over a Maine coon named Moses that neither of them had wanted. Mrs. Chandler's son Jim stood nearby, absorbed in his own memories.

In the

"I'll never understand how she knew when to show up with that kitten." Cheryl muttered, not really to anyone.

Jim turned to her with a look of surprise and a smile. "It was you!" he exclaimed. "You're the woman that Mom bought the cat for!"

"What do you mean, bought it? I thought she found it on her doorstep."

"Found it, my eye! She shopped for days—had all of us searching the paper, watching bulletin boards, calling breeders. We thought she was losing her mind—she hated cats! But she finally found him. Named him Joshua and said he was appointed to take Moses' place just like in the Bible. Kept him at her house for three days, then announced she was turning him over to his rightful owner. She must have thought very highly of you because she paid $250 for that cat—a Maine coon, she called it."

Cheryl couldn't stop fresh tears of love and gratitude from overflowing. She wished she could thank Mrs. Chandler—for Joshua, for everything. But somehow she understood that Mrs. Chandler's act of love brought greater satisfaction than a mere *thank-you* could have given.

Company of Friends

thank you for your thoughtfulness

thank you for your thoughtfulness

thank you for.

thank you for your thoughtfulness

thank you for your thoughtfulnes

thank you for your thoughtfulness

thank
you

The seeds of your

thoughtfulness

were sown in

mercy. Now the

harvest returns to

you in love.

The words of kindness are more healing to a drooping heart than balm or honey.

SARAH FIELDING

From
A Psalm of Life

Lives of great men all remind us
We can make our lives sublime,
And departing, leave behind us
Footprints on the sands of time;

Footprints, that perhaps another,
Sailing o'er life's solemn main,
A forlorn and shipwrecked brother,
Seeing, shall take heart again.

—Henry Wadsworth Longfellow

thank you for your thoughtfulness

thank you for your thoughtfulness

thank you for

thank you for your thoughtfulness

thank you for your thoughtfulness

thank you for your thoughtfulnes

thank you for your thoughtfulness

thank
you

I'll never

forget the

thoughtful

things you've

done for me.

thank
you

for your
thoughtfulness

Dear Heavenly Father,

The thoughtful ways of one special person in my life are a wonderful blessing to me. It seems few people take the time to show thoughtfulness toward others. But she still sees the value in pausing to consider others and has acted in a way that touched me deeply. This kindness is a reflection of Your kindness, and I want to thank You for the reminder of Your goodness shown through her.

Father, unsolicited acts of kindness refresh my spirit like springs of cool water on hot desert sand. I want to return this blessing, but my words are inadequate to express the impact her thoughtfulness has had on my heart. So, Lord, I ask You to bless her as only You can.

Your gracious heart was reflected in the sensitivity of this thoughtful person. I'm so thankful, Father, for this special relationship.

Amen.

MAY THE LORD
NOW SHOW YOU
KINDNESS AND
FAITHFULNESS,
AND I TOO
WILL SHOW
YOU THE
SAME FAVOR
BECAUSE
YOU HAVE
DONE THIS.

2 Samuel 2:6
NIV